Henry Percy Litchfield

The Franco-German War of 1870

Henry Percy Litchfield

The Franco-German War of 1870

ISBN/EAN: 9783337118228

Printed in Europe, USA, Canada, Australia, Japan

Cover: Foto ©ninafisch / pixelio.de

More available books at **www.hansebooks.com**

The Franco-German War of 1870

BY

HENRY PERCY LITCHFIELD

GRACEHILL
BROOKLYN, L. I.
1872

AFFECTIONATELY INSCRIBED

TO

MY FATHER

EDWIN C. LITCHFIELD

THE FRANCO-GERMAN WAR OF
1870

THE FRANCO-GERMAN WAR OF 1870

THE year 1870 opened with as fair a prospect as one apparently could wish for of the continuance of the then general European peace : and no cloud in the political horizon portended the coming struggle between two of the first-class Powers of the Continent : still less would it have been predicted that the struggle would have ended as it did.

Germany was occupied with the work of Unification. The War of 1866 had resulted in the dissolution of the old Germanic Confederation, and in the formation of two new ones (with the river Main for their common boundary) and in the exclusion of Austria from German affairs. These two confederations were known respectively as the Northern and the Southern.

The War of 1866, itself, grew out of the war with Denmark in 1864. The alleged object of this war was to deliver Holstein (a German-speaking country in the north, whose duke was the King of Denmark) from a foreign yoke. This movement began in 1863. Frederick VII. was then King of Denmark; but, dying childless in November of that year, he was succeeded by Christian IX., a prince of the House of Schleswig-Holstein, who, by virtue of a previous treaty, ascended the throne in preference to the intermediate heirs. The Holsteiners, however, refused to recognize the new King as their duke; upon which, Prince Frederic, son of the Duke of Augustinburg, claimed the duchy. The German Diet then determined that, on account of its German origin, the duchy should be separated from

Denmark. At this point, Prussia and Austria, thrusting aside the minor States, formed an alliance and commenced the war on their own account. The Danes resisted heroically, but in vain. They had hoped for the assistance of England and France, in which countries the popular feeling was favorable to their cause. The sympathy in England for the Danes was doubtless due, in a great measure, to the fact that the eldest daughter of the new King of Denmark had but recently married the Prince of Wales, and she at once became extremely popular in her adopted country. But as the Crown Prince of Prussia had some years before married the eldest daughter of Queen Victoria, and as his eldest son, the prospective King of Prussia, is the eldest grandson of that queen, it may be considered doubtful whether the Queen of England would regard the aggrandizement of Prussia at the expense of Denmark in the same light as the Princess of Wales. In any case, the French and English Governments were desirous of preserving the peace for themselves; and the Danes, left unaided, were compelled to yield to superior numbers, and to cede, not only Holstein, but also Schleswig, to the enemy. Thus Germany, after clamoring to free Holstein, a German-speaking country, from the Danish yoke, did not hesitate to impose the German yoke on Schleswig, a country inhabited by a Danish people, speaking the Danish language. The wrong, too, was inflicted by a powerful State on a weak neighbor, unable to resist.

But Prussia, ever since the accession of King William, has, in reality, been governed by his Premier, Count Bismarck, a bold and able, though unscrupulous man, whose chief object appears to be the aggrandizement of Prussia, which he would seek to accomplish by fair means or foul, and whose only thought would seem to be, how he may most firmly secure her acquisitions. He has, accordingly, been very unpopular, personally, both in and out of Germany, though his success in uniting Germany has caused considerable abatement of the feeling against him in that country.

The understanding between Prussia and Austria had been that the spoils acquired from Denmark should be equally divided between them. But, as often happens in such cases, having accomplished their object the parties disagreed as to the division of the spoils. The lust of conquest has always stained the character of the Prussian Government, as Prussian history shows; and Count Bismarck far from abandoning the policy of territorial acquisition, seems to have made it a cardinal point of his administration.

This dispute finally resulted in the War of 1866. The war lasted less than a fortnight; and its shortness and consequences excited universal astonishment in Europe. Within this fortnight, the political face of Germany was changed. Austria, which had been for centuries, the leading State of Germany, and which was esteemed a first-class Power, was signally defeated by Prussia (a comparatively new State,) and excluded from the affairs of the Confederation. New territory was added to Prussia, and Germany, with the exception of Austria, was formed into two confederations, as stated above. Part of the territory annexed to Prussia was Hanover, whose king, George V. (grandson of George III., King of both England and Hanover), unfortunately for himself, sided with Austria in this war, and lost his dominions in consequence. This war, it will be seen, increased the power of Prussia, as she became territorially and politically the leading State of Germany, and, indeed, one of the leading Powers of Europe. Her victory over Austria, though it took the world by surprise, was in reality quite natural. Austria was composed of several distinct nationalities, speaking different languages, and which, though under the same sovereign, were united by no common bond. Prussia, however, is inhabited, principally, by a population descended from a common stock with identical interests. The provinces she acquired in the partition of Poland would appear to be united and in complete harmony with the rest of Prussia. Her successes are also due to the excellency of her military institutions. Every man is something of a soldier, and liable to take the field in case of necessity.

Another result of the War of 1866 was the acquisition of Venice by Italy. Ever since the days of the Roman Empire, Italy had been divided into several independent States, at one time feudatory to the German Empire, but which in the Middle Ages became the seats of several famous republics, and the scenes of numberless wars. Italy remained divided until the movement of 1859 united the whole peninsula into one kingdom, with the exception of Rome and of the adjacent territory, which remained under the temporal sovereignty of the Pope: and of Venice, which had been an Austrian province ever since the days of the first Napoleon, and which was not taken from Austria at the same time as Lombardy, which, with the aid of France, Sardinia wrested from that monarchy in 1859. A general movement at that time throughout Italy united the greater part of the peninsula to the dominions of the Sardinian monarch (Victor Emmanuel) who thenceforth assumed the title of King of Italy. By allying herself with Prussia against Austria in 1866, Italy acquired Venice, which was ceded to her at the end of the war; and she thus only needed the remains of the Papal dominions to complete the political unity of the peninsula. The continued occupation of Rome by Napoleon III. prevented the immediate union of the city of Rome to the Italian kingdom; though it was evident that the downfall of the temporal power of the Pope was but a question of time, and that, by patiently waiting, the Italians would eventually find themselves masters of the city. The removal of the capital from Turin to Florence was regarded as a step in that direction. I have digressed so far, not because Italy took part in the War of 1870, but because the results of that war on Italy were considerable.

France, at the beginning of 1870, was in a state of high apparent prosperity. Since 1848, she had been under the government of Napoleon III., who had been elected President of the French Republic towards the end of that year, and who was elected Emperor in December, 1852. But his seat was far from easy. It is true he was elected by an immense majority of the people; but there were still partisans of the Republic in France; and also adherents of the Bourbon and Orleans dynasties. He did not marry until after he became Emperor; and at the birth of his son, the Prince Imperial, in 1856, he was already forty-eight years of age; and, consequently, his age, together with the weight of government, might have carried him off at any time before the Prince Imperial arrived at the age of manhood, and would have exposed France to another revolution and his dynasty to an overthrow. He was, of course, anxious to transmit the throne to his descendants; and the young Prince, had he been twenty years older, would have been more sure of ascending the throne.

Finally, towards the close of 1869 the Emperor seemed willing to grant some constitutional reforms,—such as, the liberty of the press, and greater freedom of discussion to the *Corps Législatif*. He accordingly appointed as Prime Minister, Émile Olivier, a man of liberal views. The *Corps Législatif* chosen in 1869 contained among its members Gambetta and Rochefort. The former became, before a year had passed, one of the foremost men of France. The latter had acquired his celebrity, not from any inherent ability that he possessed, but on account of the violent antagonism he had shown to the Emperor, several years before, in a journal of which he was editor, and which had then caused his banishment. He took advantage of the recent amnesty of the Emperor to all French exiles to return to France in 1869 and was elected to the *Corps Législatif* by a district comprising the lowest class of the Parisian population, who probably supposed that his having been banished, together with his inveterate hostility to the Emperor, proved his competency for the Legislature.

He took his seat in the Legislature and continued his attacks on the Emperor. But an event occurred early in 1870, which caused great agitation in Paris, and endangered the safety of the Government. Victor Noir, not only one of the partisans of Rochefort, but also one of the assistants in editing his paper, called upon Prince Pierre Bonaparte, a cousin of the Emperor. The real object of the visit will probably never be known: but it seems to have had a suspicious appearance; for the Prince, in a heat of passion killed him. The excitement that followed in consequence of this event was immense but was successfully put down; and the *plebiscite* of the following May seemed to establish the Emperor more firmly on his throne.

A war between France and Prussia seemed a possibility of the remote future, though a possibility which must, sooner or later, become a reality. But the event was nearer than people supposed, and the spark that lighted the war came from a quarter whence it was least expected. Breaking out as it did in the midst of profound peace, it shows how difficult it is to foretell an event a short time before it happens.

Spain, in the southwest of Europe had been governed, since the beginning of the eighteenth century, by a younger branch of the Bourbon dynasty. The concentration of all political power into the hands of the King, together with the degeneracy of the last monarchs of that family, had caused Spain to decline in prosperity. The misgovernment of the last queen, Isabella II., resulting from a bad education and evil counsellors, led to the Revolution of 1868, when Queen Isabella was driven from the kingdom, and the throne declared vacant.

General Prim became the head of Government, and he continued to be the real ruler of the nation until his death (caused by assassination, on New Year's Day, 1871, in the fifty-seventh year of his age) notwithstanding that, after the Cortes had decided in favor of a monarchy, Serrano, under the title of Regent, became the nominal chief of the Government.

Queen Isabella and her family fled

to Paris, where they were received by the Emperor Napoleon; but they lived there very privately. In the meantime, it being decided that monarchical institutions should be maintained in Spain, the election of a monarch for that country became the practical question of the hour, and excited much interest in Europe. Several candidates were brought forward and rejected for various reasons. In the summer of 1870, General Prim offered the crown of Spain to a German prince of the House of Hohenzollern, distantly related to the King of Prussia; and he summoned the Cortes to meet about the middle of July for the purpose of electing him. The Prince at first accepted the offer; but no sooner was his nomination known in France, than Frenchmen of all parties pronounced the election of a German prince to the throne of Spain an insult to their country; and they declared that the recent nomination had been premeditated by Count Bismarck for the purpose of annoying France, and of acquiring an ally for Germany in the South, in case a war should break out between France and Prussia.

Since the dethronement of Queen Isabella, in September, 1868, Europe, generally, had taken considerable interest in the question, "Who shall be King of Spain?" It was about two years before a suitable candidate was found. Queen Isabella's renunciation of the throne of Spain in favor of her son, the Prince of the Asturias, was not much heeded. The ex-King of Portugal refused the crown *in toto*. Espartero, a Spanish general, though he had some partisans, would not have answered, as he was already very old, and he had no children to whom the throne might descend; the other candidates were foreign princes, and were rejected, either on account of their youth, or from deference to the Emperor Napoleon.

It is difficult to conceive how the news of the nomination of the Prince of Hohenzollern to the throne of Spain could have roused the French to such a pitch of frenzy, for he was as eligible as any of the candidates proposed; neither would his election have been more threatening than that of the others—for it would have been more necessary to his interest as king to seat himself firmly on the throne by ingratiating himself in the affections of his subjects, than to form an offensive and defensive alliance with his native country. But his German nationality prejudiced the French against him, and brought on the war. We give extracts below from several Parisian journals, showing the state of feeling in France on the subject.

The *Constitutionnel* observed:

"The sentiments produced on our mind by the candidature of the Prince of Hohenzollern for the crown of Spain, are shared by most of our contemporaries, there being a general feeling of doubt, astonishment, and suspense. It appears that the Spaniards are about in the same case, although so deeply interested in the affair. It is true that they still preserve a hope of being consulted. A Madrid journal, the *Tiempo*, declares that the Prussian candidate, upheld by several ministers, fifteen or twenty deputies, and Marshal Prim, will see formed against him a league, composed of Republicans, Carlists, Montpensierists, and the partisans of Alphonso XII.,—that is to say,—everybody. The same organ, however, adds that the question is not so far advanced as has been imagined; that the present Government has contracted no formal engagement, and that the Prussian Prince puts conditions on his acceptance which will not perhaps be acceded to. It seems to us, indeed, very improbable that Marshal Prim, who has always piqued himself on a profound respect for the national will, would at once overleap it so abruptly, and suppress it. It may also be remarked, that at present, much is said of the Prince's relationship, and little of himself, personally. His allies and ancestors are known and that is all. Who is he? What is he fit for? What are his ideas? If the people revolt against legitimate and semi-legitimate rulers, against divine right, it is not, doubtless, for the purpose of choosing fresh princes, guided solely by the sacred pages of the Almanac de Gotha. Either the future King of Spain is only to play the modest part of a master of the ceremonies, in which case it will not be worth while to be so long on the lookout; or, he is really destined to exercise a considerable influence over the country of his adoption, in which event it would perhaps be well to discuss a little the trifling matter as to whether he is capable of doing what is expected of him."

The following is from the *Memorial Diplomatique*.

"The present is not the first time that this candidature has been brought forward. In fact, some weeks since, we assigned reasons for the matter falling through. To-day, less than ever, would King William, in his quality as head of the Hohenzollern family, authorize a Prussian prince to accept that crown which Queen Isabella has just abdicated in favor of her son, the Prince of the Asturias. Let the words pronounced by King William at the time of his coronation at Koenigsberg be borne in mind. After taking up his position as a resolute defender of the principle of Legitimacy, he is not a monarch who would allow a member of his family to usurp a crown in connivance with the Revolution."

The *Nord* says:

"The probability is, that the part taken by Count Bismarck in the candidature of Prince Leopold has been singularly exaggerated. That the latter has accepted the offer of Marshal

Prim is probable; that King William, whose authorization is necessary, has consented, may also be true; but the fact seems to be more than doubtful that the Prussian Government consented eagerly to the wishes of the Spanish Prime Minister. One quality which no one can deny to the Federal chancellor is practical common sense; and endowed as he is with that faculty, he could not help seeing the difficulty in which his country would almost inevitably be involved by the accession of a prince of its royal house to the throne of Spain. The stability of the new Peninsular dynasty would be far from secure."

The *Débats* observed on this subject:

"As we do not suppose that Prim, if he had been carrying on an intrigue, would have had the kindness to impart to the correspondent of the *Agency* an answer to his question, in order that he might inform the whole of Europe, we do not attach the slightest importance to the denials of the telegraph. What is rather more serious in the despatch of which we speak, is the fact that it contradicts the statement of there being an intention of proclaiming a king without the approval of the Cortes, given, not by a simple, but by an absolute majority, in conformity with the law recently voted. It must be confessed, that if there had been an attempt to go to work in any other way, as the first telegram seemed to indicate, and to impose Prince Leopold on Spain, without having first consulted the representatives of the country, it would have appeared more as if those in authority were seeking to light up the flames of civil war, than to find a king for this throne, vacant now for nearly two years."

The *Avenir National* spoke thus:

"Prince Leopold is not only a firm Catholic, but of a pleasant disposition, and little inclined to opposition. He will be, in Prim's hands, an instrument not less docile than his brother has been for the various ministers who have succeeded each other at Bucharest, since his accession to the throne of the Danubian Principalities. He is just the candidate for a minister who is ambitious, and anxious to hold sway. Another advantage that this pretender would have in Prim's eyes is, that, in his quality of eldest son, he would one day inherit a fortune, considerable even for a prince. He is not a younger brother, as the *Patria* has it. The fervor of the Catholic sentiments of the Hohenzollern-Sigmaringen family did not prevent it from enriching itself with the property of the abbeys in the beginning of the century. Besides, Napoleon I. behaved very generously to the grandfather when this latter married a Murat princess, as he generally did to the members of the royal houses who consented to form alliances with his family. Finally, the cession of the Principality with its forty thousand inhabitants made by the father to the King of Prussia in the midst of the troubles of 1849, did not take place without a heavy pecuniary indemnity in the shape of a very high annual income which the Prussian Treasury pays every year. Prim would have shown only an ill-grace had he presented to the Spanish people a Pretender insufficiently provided for, needy, and on his knees for a five-franc piece, as Beaumarchais has it. Evidently, he who casts a doubt on the pecuniary resources of the candidate was misled by the moderate means of the reigning family in Prussia. Prim's *protégé* is in no way like the other princes of that country, being of an unwarlike disposition, a fervent Catholic, studious, and rich, whilst his cousins are soldiers from head to foot, Protestants, not very deeply lettered, and with small fortunes.''

These extracts would appear to show that the feeling of France generally was opposed to the election of a Prussian Prince to the throne of Spain, notwithstanding the fact that the candidate was more nearly related, through females, to the Emperor Napoleon, than to the King of Prussia. It would hardly be worth while to bring the candidature so prominently into notice, but for the fact of its instrumentality in bringing on a war which led to the most important results to the countries engaged, and which led indirectly to other results of equal importance to the world at large. I will refer to these in the proper place.

The father of Prince Leopold renounced in behalf of his son all claims to the throne of Spain as soon as he saw the difficulties it would give rise to in Europe; but the renunciation did not have the desired effect. The nomination of the Prince was made known to Europe, July 5, 1870; a week after, on the 12th, he notified the French Government of his renunciation. This renunciation was apparently as satisfactory as could be desired ; but it was not enough. The King of Prussia was staying at the time at the watering-place of Ems ; and on the morning of the 13th, he was met by M. Benedetti, the French Ambassador, on the Promenade. The King handed M. Benedetti a Cologne newspaper, containing the news of the Prince's renunciation. This, M. Benedetti said he already knew. On the King's saying the matter was finally settled, Benedetti made the unexpected demand for a distinct assurance from that monarch that his consent would never be given to the candidature, if it should be made in future, which assurance the King firmly refused to give, though repeatedly urged to do so by the French Ambassador. The King, later in the day, denied an interview to Benedetti, on the ground that his final answer was already given, and giving him to understand that communications must proceed regularly through his ministers. On the following day, the French Ambassador left Ems, after taking an informal leave of the King.

On the 15th, M. Olivier, Prime Minister of the Emperor Napoleon, announced to the *Corps Législatif* the determination of the Government to break off all diplomatic intercourse with Prussia. In this communication, after giving an account of the negotiations, the Premier added: "Under these circumstances, the Government would have forgotten its dignity, and also its prudence, had it not made preparations. We have prepared to maintain the war which is offered to us, leaving upon each that portion of the responsibility which devolves upon him. Since yesterday, we have called out the reserves, and we shall take necessary measures to guard the interests, the security, and the honor of France."

This address was generally accepted, not merely by the *Corps Législatif*, but by Europe, as a declaration of war, as it virtually was; for it showed that the war had been definitely decided upon by the French Government, though the formal declaration was delayed some days longer. On the day this address was delivered, the Duc de Grammont, the Minister of Foreign Affairs, told the English Ambassador in Paris, that the "Prussian Government had deliberately insulted France, by declaring to the public that the King had affronted the French Ambassador. It was evidently the intention of the Government of Prussia to take credit with the people of Germany for having acted with haughtiness and discourtesy: in fact, to humiliate France." On the 20th, the Duke, in a speech to the *Corps Législatif*, said: "In conformity with the law or custom, and by order of the Emperor, I have requested the French *Chargé d'Affaires* at the Court of Berlin to notify to the Prussian Government our resolution to seek by force of arms the guaranties we have not been able to obtain by discussion. That step has been taken, and I have the honor to inform the Legislative Body, that consequently, a state of war exists since yesterday, the 19th, between France and Prussia. This declaration also applies to the allies of Prussia, who lend to that Power the assistance of their arms against us."

The Declaration of War sent to Berlin was in the following terms:

"In fulfilment of the orders he has received from his government, the undersigned *Chargé d'Affaires* of France has the honor to make known to his Excellency the Minister of Foreign Affairs to his Majesty the King of Prussia, the following communication: The Government of his Majesty, the Emperor of the French, not being able to regard the design of raising a Prussian Prince to the Throne of Spain, as anything but an enterprise directed against the territorial security of France, found itself under the necessity of requiring from his Majesty the King of Prussia an assurance that such a combination should not be carried into effect without his consent. His Majesty, the King of Prussia, refused to give the assurance, and stated, on the contrary, to the Ambassador of his Majesty the Emperor, that he reserved to himself for that eventuality, as in all others, the power of taking account of circumstances. The Imperial Government could not but perceive in that declaration on the part of the King, reservations which were threatening for France and the general balance of power in Europe. A second fact gave still more gravity to that declaration : The announcement made to all the Cabinets of Europe of the refusal to receive the Emperor's Ambassador or to enter into further conferences with him. In consequence, the French Government felt it to be a duty to take steps for the immediate defence of its honor and interests, and to adopt all the measures required by the position of affairs. Consequently, from this time it considers itself in a state of war with Prussia.

Le Sourde."

The Premier also sent circulars to the archbishops and bishops of the Roman Church; and to the heads of the Reformed Churches, requiring prayers to be offered up for the success of the French arms. The circular ran as follows:

"Monseigneur: I request you in the name of his Majesty, to order public prayers in your diocese. Put France, and her Chief, and the noble child about to go to war before the required age, under the protection of Him who holds in His hands the ordering of battles and the destinies of nations. And at the moment that our heroic army sets out on its march, pray God that He will bless our arms, and that He will permit a glorious and durable peace soon to succeed to the pains and the sufferings caused by war.

"Accept, Monseigneur, the assurance of my high esteem.
"Émile Olivier."

The above document was dated July 26, 1870.

The circular addressed to the Reformed Churches was slightly different from the above.

The Legislative Body made the following address to the Emperor Napoleon on the occasion of declaring war: its President, M. Schneider, acting as spokesman:

"Sire: The Legislative Body has terminated its labor, after voting all the subsidies and laws necessary for the defence of the country. Thus the Chamber has united in an effective proof of patriotism. The real author of war is not he by whom it is declared, but he who renders it necessary. There will be but one voice among the people of both hemispheres, throwing the responsibility upon Prussia, which, intoxicated by unexpected success, and encouraged by our patience and our desire to preserve to Europe the blessings of peace, has imagined that she could conspire against our security and wound our honor with impunity. Under these circumstances, France will know how to do her duty. The most ardent wishes will follow you to the army, the command of which you assume, accompanied by your son, who, anticipating the duties of maturer age, will learn, by your side, how to serve his country. Behind you—behind our army, accustomed to carry the noble flag of France—stands the whole nation ready to recruit it. Leave the Regency, without anxiety, in the hands of our august Sovereign, the Empress. To the authority commanded by her great qualities, of which ample evidence has already been given, her Majesty will add the strength now afforded by the liberal institutions so gloriously inaugurated by your Majesty. Sire, the heart of the whole nation is with you, and with your valiant army."

The Emperor made the following reply:

"I experience the most lively satisfaction, on the eve of my departure for the army, at being able to thank you for the patriotic support which you have afforded my government. A war is right when it is waged with the assent of the country, and the approval of the country's representatives. You do right to remember the words of Montesquieu, that 'the real author of war is not he by whom it is declared, but he who renders it necessary.' We have done all in our power to avert the war, and I may say that it is the whole nation that has, by its irresistible impulses, dictated our decisions. I confide to you the Empress, who will call you around her, if circumstances should require it. She will know how to fulfil courageously the duty which her position imposes upon her. I take my son with me: in the midst of the army he will learn to serve his country. Resolved energetically to pursue the great mission which has been entrusted to me, I have faith in the success of our arms: for I know that behind me France has arisen to her feet, and that God protects her."

On July 20th, the French Government issued the following declaration concerning Prussian interests in France:

"The Emperor has determined, on the suggestion of his Excellency, the Minister for Foreign Affairs, that the subjects of Prussia, and of the allies affording her armed assistance against us, who are now in France or her colonies, shall be allowed to remain as long as their conduct affords no grounds for complaint.

"The admission into French territory of subjects of Prussia and her allies, is from the present date subject to special authorizations, which shall only be granted exceptionally.

"With regard to the enemy's merchant vessels now in the ports of the Empire, or which may enter them in ignorance of the state of war, his Majesty has been pleased to order that they shall be allowed a period of thirty days to leave those ports. Safe conducts will be given to them to enable them freely to return to those ports to which they belong, or to go direct to the port of their destination.

"Vessels which shall have shipped cargoes for French ports, and on French account in the enemy's or neutral ports previous to the declaration of war, are not subjects to capture. They may freely discharge their freight in the ports of the Empire, and will receive safe conducts to return to the ports to which they belong."

The King of Prussia opened the Parliament of the North-German Confederation in person on the 19th of July, and, in a speech from the throne he informed the House of the rupture with France. Information of the declaration of war was given to Count Bismarck on the same day. The Parliament, in reply, made the following address :

"Most Serene Lord ! Most Gracious King and Sovereign !

"The sublime words which your Majesty has addressed to us in the name of the Confederated Governments, meet with a powerful response among the German people.

"One thought, one will, moves the German heart at this moment.

"The nation is filled with joyous pride at the great sternness and high honor with which your Majesty treated the unheard-of demands of the enemy, who thought to humble us, and who invades the Fatherland with ill-considered pretexts.

"The German people have no other wish than to live in peace and friendship with all nations that respect the honor and independence of Germany.

"As in the celebrated times of the wars of independence, so does Napoleon force us again to-day into sacred strife for our rights and liberties.

"All calculations of the moral force and determined will of the German people, based upon the meanness and perfidy of mankind, are now, as formerly, brought into disgrace.

"That portion of the French people, led astray through jealousy and ambition, will learn too late the terrible results that await all nations that engage in bloody strife.

"The cautious policy of our people has not succeeded in preventing the crime directed against the welfare of the French, and the friendly relations of the two nations.

"Germany knows that a great and terrible conflict awaits her.

"We confide in the bravery and patriotism of our armed brethren, on the unshaken determination of a united people, to venture all temporal goods, and not to suffer the foreign conqueror to bend the neck of the German citizen.

"We confide in the guidance of the gray hero-king, the German general whom Providence has appointed to lead to a decisive end in the evening of his life the great struggle which he fought as a youth, half a century ago.

"We trust in God, whose justice punishes bloody transgressions.

"From the shores of the seas to the foot of the Alps the people have risen at the call of their patriotic princes.

"No sacrifice is too great for them.

"Public opinion throughout the world recognizes the justice of our cause.

"Friendly nations behold in our victory their deliverance from the weighty oppression of the Bonaparte domination and the expiation of the wrongs perpetrated on them.

"The German people will finally find on the victorious battle-field—ground valued by all nations—a more peaceful and independent unity.

"Your Majesty and the Confederated Governments find us prepared, like our brethren in the South.

"It touches your honor and our freedom.

"It touches the tranquillity of Europe, and the welfare of the people.

"In deep reverence we remain,
  "Your royal Majesty,
  "Most loyally and faithfully,
    "The *Reichstag* of the North German Confederation."

The King, before leaving for the war, issued the following proclamation:

"I am compelled to draw the sword in consequence of a wanton attack, which must be warded off with all the strength at the command of Germany. It is a great consolation to me before God and man, that I have not in any way given occasion for the onslaught. My conscience is clear as to the right of this war, and I am confident before God of the justice of our cause. The conflict is earnest, and it will entail heavy sacrifices on my people, and on Germany at large. But I depart for war, looking up to an all-knowing God, and appealing to His all-powerful help. Already I have occasion to thank God that, at the first whisper of war, all German hearts were animated by one feeling : a feeling of indignation at the attack, and of glad trustfulness that God would grant victory to the rightful cause. My people will stand by me in this conflict as they stood by my father, who now rests in God. With me they will make any sacrifice to restore peace to the nations. From my youth up I have learnt to confide in the omnipotence of God's gracious help. In Him I hope, and I call on my people to have a like confidence in Him. I bow before God in acknowledgment of His mercy, and I am convinced that my subjects will do likewise. For this reason, I appoint that Wednesday, the 27th of July, be kept as an extraordinary general day of prayer, when Divine service will be held in the churches, and public business shall be suspended in so far as the pressing necessity of the time shall permit. I also appoint that, during the continuance of the war, in every public Divine service, prayers shall be offered up that God may lead us to victory, that He may be merciful even to our enemies, and that He may graciously conduct us to a peace that will secure the honor and the lasting independence of Germany.

"WILLIAM.

"BERLIN, July 21, 1870."

The leading states of Europe declared themselves neutral. Belgium, Holland, and Switzerland at first sent troops to their frontiers to defend their neutrality. Some excitement was created by the alleged discovery of a secret treaty between France and Prussia—before the war had fairly begun—said to have been drawn up in 1864, in which France agreed not to oppose the unification of Germany, while the Prussians were to support France in annexing the kingdom of Belgium and the Grand Duchy of Luxembourg. The difficulty in accounting for this treaty was, that it was in the handwriting of Benedetti (the French Ambassador at the Court of Berlin), and in the possession of Bismarck, which gave it an appearance of genuineness. But the indifferent French of the original, combined with other mistakes, caused its genuineness to be doubted. Bismarck maintained that Benedetti offered to make such a treaty with Prussia, on behalf of the French Government; while Benedetti affirmed that one day, being in conversation with Bismarck, at his request, he (Benedetti) took down the heads of a treaty, and left it with him. This, however, is a digression, as the subject did not loom up again during the war.

At the end of July, the hostile armies were moving to the frontiers of France and Germany and each was nominally commanded by its respective sovereign in person. The South German States had, after a momentary hesitation, declared their adhesion to the national cause ; so that Germany now presented an unbroken front to the French.

The Emperor Napoleon issued the following proclamation at Metz, July 28th, on taking the command of the Army of the Rhine :

"I place myself at your head, to defend the honor of the nation. You will fight one of the best armies in Europe : though other armies, equally able, could not withstand you. The struggle will to-day be equal. The war will be long and painful, but nothing surpasses the tenacious bravery of the soldiers who fought in Africa, in the Crimea, in Italy, and in Mexico. Whichever way we turn, beyond the boundaries of our country, we find continually the glorious footsteps of our forefathers, and we will show ourselves worthy of them. All France follows you with her best wishes; the world has its eyes fixed upon you; upon your success hang the destinies of freedom and civilization. Let each one do his duty, and the God of Battles will be on our side!"

Each belligerent thus claimed to be fighting for right, justice, and liberty.

Before leaving Paris, the Emperor had appointed his consort, the Empress, Regent of the Empire during his absence. He was accompanied to the theatre of war by the Prince Imperial, a boy of fourteen, whom he wished to accustom to war.

War of 1870

Under the French Emperor were three marshals, who were probably the real leaders of the army. Foremost among these was Marshal MacMahon. He was of Irish extraction, and was born in 1808; he was consequently sixty-two years of age at the outbreak of the war. He had already served in Africa and the Crimea, and likewise in Lombardy. Marshal Canrobert, born in 1809, who took command of the Sixth Corps, had served in Algeria, and, as a general of division, in the Crimean War. The Second and Fifth Corps were commanded respectively by Froissard and Failly. Marshal Bazaine, who took command of the Fourth Corps, had served in Mexico.

The King of Prussia took the field in person at the head of his army; but the real director of the military movements was Count von Moltke, a Dane by birth, and a veteran of long experience, who continued till the end of the war the chief military adviser of the Prussian monarch. The Crown

Prince of Prussia was appointed to the command of the South German contingents. Prince Frederic Charles,— the King's nephew, known as the Red Prince,—Von Rittenfeld, Von Falkenstein, Manteuffel, and Steinmetz, were among the other principal commanders. Some of them were born in the times of the French Revolution. Count Bismarck also followed the army, though he took no command.

Germany was able to put in the field 1,100,000 men; France was able to put in the field only 600,000 men. Though the military force of Germany was thus nearly double that of France, yet, as the Southern states wavered for a moment, it was expected that the French generals would take advantage of this hesitation, by making a sudden raid into Southern Germany, thereby alienating them from Prussia. This might have secured Austria (still smarting under the defeat of 1866) and Italy. It was in general looked upon as a matter of course that the French arms would be successful in the beginning of the war, even by many who thought they would not be ultimately successful. Had the French Emperor been able to follow out this plan, he might have influenced in a great measure the subsequent course of the war. For a week or more after the French Emperor had issued his proclamation to the army, all Europe was awaiting the movements of the hostile armies with breathless anxiety.

In the meantime, the German troops, both of the Northern and Southern Confederations, were enabled to assemble; and soon after the 1st of August, they were all at the seat of war. The two armies stood confronting each other all along the frontier of France and Germany between Switzerland and Belgium.

Before the actual outbreak of hostilities, the Prussians blew up the railway bridge between Strasburg and Kehl, on the Rhine; thereby preventing the bridge from being used for the transport of French troops across the Rhine.

It was afterwards explained that the continued inaction of the Emperor Napoleon was due to the fact that the forces on which he was counting were not forthcoming, thus forcing him to remain in Metz longer than he intended. He had at first proposed marching with 250,000 men that were to have assembled at Metz and Strasburg into Southern Germany in order to secure the neutrality of that Confederation; after which they were to march against the Prussians. In the meantime, 50,000 men under Marshal Canrobert were to protect the northeastern frontier. In point of fact, only 100,000 had assembled at Metz, and 40,000 at Strasburg, instead of 150,000 which were awaited at the former place, and 100,000 at the latter.

On the 2d of August the first shot of the campaign was fired by a French division, under General Bataille, who attacked and carried the

Heights of Spicheren, in the neighborhood of Saarbruck, a Prussian town near the frontier. The battle lasted about three hours. The Prussians retired upon their next line of defence: the French, after the battle, appear to have withdrawn across their own border to Metz. Some importance was attached to this battle, as it was fought in the presence of the Emperor and the Prince Imperial ; the latter was said to have received his *baptism of fire* in this battle. This success, small as it was, was almost the only one on the French side during the whole course of the war.

For the German forces being assembled about this time, they took the offensive soon after the battle of Saarbruck, and advanced into the French territory. The Crown Prince of Prussia, with 40,000 men under him, advanced upon Weissenburg, a French town near the frontier, in which neighborhood they found a division of the French army under General Douay. The division consisted of the 74th and

50th regiments of the line, the 16th battalion of foot, a regiment of Turcos, and one of mounted Chasseurs. The Crown Prince came upon them unexpectedly on the morning of the 4th, and at once attacked them. The French fought vigorously, and maintained the unequal conflict (the Prussians having the advantage of numbers) during the greater part of the day; leaving tents, baggage, etc. in the hands of the enemy, they lost 800 prisoners, and had their commander, Douay, killed in the field.

Marshal MacMahon, commander-in-chief of the army to which this division belonged, was then at Metz, attending a council of war; he no sooner heard of the French defeat than he hastened to join his army, and with 50,000 men encamped near Woerth, a little farther in the interior of France than Weissenburg.

The Crown Prince advanced with 130,000 troops from Weissenburg, and attacked MacMahon on the 6th. The battle was fought with great vigor on both sides, and ended, like the former, in the total rout and defeat of the French, who lost 10,000 men put *hors de combat*, and 7000 taken prisoners: 4000 being taken in battle, and the remainder during the pursuit. The German loss was 7000 put *hors de combat*.

On that same day, Saarbruck was evacuated by the French. A battle fought on the Heights of Spicheren, near Saarbruck, resulted, likewise, in the defeat of the French: but in this case, the French had the numerical advantage. The French army concentrated in Metz on the 10th.

During this time, great commotion prevailed in Paris. A report was circulated on the 6th that Marshal MacMahon had gained a great victory over the Germans, and had captured the Crown Prince and his army. This caused great excitement: but when it was found that the news was false, a reaction set in. The defeat of the

French was announced by telegram by the Emperor Napoleon, who added: "All may yet be well." These events resulted in the resignation of the Olivier Ministry, and in the formation of a new one, with Count Pelikas as Premier. The premiership of the Count was necessarily short-lived, being overthrown with the Empire in September. The demand of the people for arms, was complied with, and the Department of the Seine was at once declared in a state of siege. The great excitement that prevailed also made the populace suspicious of strangers, and the cry of "spy" was continually raised against foreigners, and it was as continually proving false.

The defeats of the French were made known to them by the Ministers in Paris, in the following proclamation:

"FRENCHMEN! We have told you the whole truth: it is now for you to do your duty. Let one single cry issue from the breasts of all, from one end of France to the other. Let the whole people rise, quivering, and sworn to fight the great fight. Some of our regiments have succumbed to overwhelming numbers, but our army has not been vanquished. The same intrepid breath still animates it : let us support it. To a momentarily successful audacity, we will oppose a union which conquers destiny. Let us fall back upon ourselves, and our invaders shall hurl themselves against a rampart of human breasts. As in 1792 and at Sebastapol, let our reverses be the school of our victories. It would be a crime to doubt for an instant the safety of our country, and a greater still not to do our part to secure it. Up, then, up! and you, inhabitants of the Centre, the North, and the South, upon whom the burden of the war does not fall, hasten with unanimous enthusiasm to the rescue of your brethren in the East. Let France, united in success, be still more united in adversity. And may God bless our arms."

The Government followed up this proclamation by active measures for the prosecution of the war. They asked for more men, calling out all citizens under forty for the services of the National Guards who were to defend the capital, and repair the fortifications. The people seem to have been confident as to the ultimate issue of the war, as the following extract, taken from a Parisian journal after the first defeat, shows :

"There exist in the life of nations solemn and decisive moments in which God gives them an opportunity of showing what they are and of what they are capable. That hour has come for France. It has sometimes been asserted that, though intrepid in the dash of success, the great nation supports reverses with difficulty. What is now passing before us gives the lie to this calumny. The attitude of the people is not one of discouragement : it is one of sublime and patriotic rage against the invaders of France, who in France must find a tomb.

"All Frenchmen will rise, like one man: they remember their ancestors and their children: behind them they see centuries of glory: before them a future that their heroism shall render free and powerful. Never before has our country been better prepared for self-devotion and sacrifice: never has it shown in a more imposing and magnificent manner the vigor and pride of the national character. It shouts with enthusiasm: 'Up! To arms!' 'To conquer or to die,' is its motto.

"While our soldiers heroically defend the soil of France, Europe is justly uneasy at the successes of Prussia. People ask themselves to what lengths the ambition of that insatiable Power would carry her, if she were intoxicated with a decisive triumph.

"It is an invariable law of history, that any nation which, by unbounded covetousness, disturbs the general equilibrium, challenges a reaction against its victories, and turns all other countries into opponents. This truth cannot fail to be demonstrated by the results. Who is interested in the resurrection of the German Empire? Who desires the Baltic to become a Prussian lake? Can it be Sweden, Norway, or Denmark? countries that a Prussian triumph would annihilate! Can it be Russia — Russia, which is interested more than any other Power in saving the equilibrium of the North against German covetousness? Can it be England, which, as a great maritime Power, and as the protector of Denmark, is opposed to the progress of the Prussian navy? Can it be Holland, which is already so much threatened by the audacious intrigues of Count Bismarck? With regard to Austria, the restoration of the German Empire to the advantage of the House of Hohenzollern would be the most fatal blow, not only to the dynasty of the Hapsburgs, but to the existence of the Austro-Hungarian Monarchy. Prussia will certainly attempt to make promises to the Cabinet of Vienna : but it is well known what faith can be placed in the word of Count Bismarck. Can any pretended guaranty ever be stronger than the ties which united Prussia to the Germanic Confederation, and which Prussia, contemning all her duties, and obligations, so violently tore asunder? The decisive victory of the Hohenzollerns would not be less fatal to Italy than to Austria. A Germanic Empire would at any price wish to acquire a sea-board. It would want one in the south as well as in the north, and would demand Venice and Trieste, as well as Kiel and Amsterdam. Thus the regeneration of Italy would be compromised.

"We appeal with confidence to the wisdom of governments and nations to root Prussian despotism out of Europe, to aid us, either by alliance or sympathy, in saving the European equilibrium. There is good ground already for noting the favorable symptoms apparent in England, which country is fully satisfied with the declarations we have so categorically and loyally given with regard to Belgian neutrality, protecting as it does our northern frontier, and which she shows herself ready to defend, on the side of Belgium, should Prussia wish to violate that country's territory. Sweden, Norway, and Denmark show an attitude trembling with patriotism. The Emperor of Russia honors our Ambassador with his particular good will, and the best authorized organs of the Russian press hold a language unfavorable to the Prussian cause. Those Vienna journals which at first timidly manifested some sympathy with Count Bismarck are compelled to give way before public opinion, and now speak in terms harmonizing with the true interests of Austria. The Emperor Francis Joseph, the King of Italy, and their governments, manifest dispositions more and more satisfactory towards us. Austria and Italy are actively arming. The Ministers of Vienna and Pesth obey a united impulse, and the moment approaches when Prussia will encounter from that quarter the most serious and grave embarrassments. Our diplomacy will not be less active than our army. France is making a supreme effort, and our patriotism rises equal to every danger. The more serious the circumstances, so much the more will the nation be energetic. All divisions cease, and the French press unanimously expresses the most practical and the most noble ideas.

"The concurrence of the Senate and the Legislative Body is about to lend fresh strength to our troops : and the French of 1870 will show the people of Europe that we have not degenerated."

At the beginning of the war each of the belligerents was confident of being ultimately victorious. The French had no doubt of success ; and it was generally supposed, from their acknowledged military superiority, and the impetuosity of their character, that, on whichever side the fortune of war should ultimately incline, the French would have the advantage of the first victories.

But no sooner had the war fairly begun, than victory after victory was announced on the German side. One army, commanded by the King of Prussia in person, and Count von Moltke, followed the French Imperial Army, commanded by the Emperor. While the French army was being driven by the enemy into the interior, and was keeping near the frontier, the Army of Southern Germany, under the command of the Crown Prince, struck into the interior; but its progress was kept more secret than that of the army commanded by the King.

The French army continued its retreat. Resigning the command of the troops stationed at Metz to Marshal Bazaine, the Emperor retired to the camp at Châlons. During the third week of August, three battles were fought in the vicinity of Metz. The Prussians attacked the French in the neighborhood of Courcelles, a small village at some distance from Metz, on the 14th. The losses on both sides were immense : and both sides claimed the victory. On the 16th the Third Prussian Corps attacked the French troops, who were commanded by Froissard. Notwithstanding their enormous loss, which amounted to 16,000 men, the Germans gained the victory, capturing 7 guns, 2000 prisoners, and driving Bazaine back seven miles towards Gravelotte. Here, on the 17th and 18th, a third and equally decisive battle, favorable to the Prussians, was fought between the two armies.

The result of these battles was to blockade Marshal Bazaine and his troops in Metz, from the 22d of August until the end of October. In order to prevent MacMahon, who, at the head of 100,000 men, was to advance to the relief of Bazaine, from taking up a defensive position to the north of Châlons, a considerable portion of the German army, under the Crown Princes of Saxony and Prussia, was sent to hold him in check. MacMahon took up his position in the Vaux, where, on the 30th of August, he was attacked by the enemy, and defeated, with the loss of 7000 men and 20 guns. He and his army, with the Emperor, then retreated to Sedan.

Next to the siege of Paris, that of Sedan must be regarded as the most important of the war, not in its length (it was of short duration), but in the magnitude of its results. The same fatality that followed the French army since the beginning of the war was against it at Sedan. On September 1st, a general action took place around Sedan, the French being defeated: 20,000 prisoners were taken by the enemy; thousands fled across the Belgian frontier. In these conflicts, Mac-Mahon himself, was wounded; being unable to retain his command in consequence, the leadership of the French forces was assumed, early on the 2d, by Wimpffen, who had hurried from Africa for the purpose. He was obliged that same day to sign a capitulation, surrendering his whole army —80,000 in all—as prisoners of war to the Germans.

The Emperor Napoleon is said to have exposed his person in these conflicts round Sedan, evidently courting death. On the 2d, the day of the capitulation, he sent his sword to the King of Prussia, requesting an interview. The interview was held at the Château of Frenois, after the signing of the capitulation. The French monarch refused to discuss politics, declaring that the Germans must treat with the Empress Regent and the Government at Paris, who, as his representatives, had full powers to sign a treaty; he also declared that his surrender was purely personal. The King appointed him his residence at

Wilhelmshoehe Palace, formerly the dwelling of the Electors of Cassel, and also, in the reign of Napoleon I., of the King of Westphalia, uncle of Napoleon III. The Emperor left for the palace on September 3d.

The news of this event was not long in being confirmed. It reached Paris on the 4th, and caused great excitement. A crowd of the populace rushed into the hall where the *Corps Législatif* was sitting, and demanded the proclamation of the Republic. The President of the *Corps Législatif* left the chair, and most of the members left the House. Those who remained exhorted the people to respect the freedom of legislative deliberation: but the only answer was, "*Vive la République!*" The surrender of the Emperor was repudiated by the crowd, among whom was repeatedly heard the cry, "An Emperor dies, but does not surrender!" Finally the crowd and the remaining members of the House dispersed, and at four that same afternoon, the Republic was proclaimed from the steps of the Hôtel de Ville, before an immense crowd, by M. Gambetta, a member of the *Corps Législatif*, and always a staunch Republican. Gambetta at once leaped into notice, and became the virtual ruler of France for the remainder of the war, as a member of the Provisional Government, which was installed on September 4th ; it contained the following members :

General TROCHU, President of the Council ; M. GAMBETTA, Minister of the Interior ; JULES FAVRE, Minister of Foreign Affairs ; COUNT KERATRY, Prefect of Police ; JULES SIMON, ROCHEFORT, JULES FERRY, ERNEST PICARD, ERNEST PELLETAN, and ARAGE, Mayor of Paris. Trochu had been appointed by the Emperor Military Governor of Paris, and a few days before the events spoken of above, he had refused the appointment of Dictator of France tendered him by the Legislature, on the ground that existing circumstances did not permit it: though he afterwards acted in concert with the Republic, and retained his post as Military Governor of Paris throughout the war. Rochefort, whose name appears as a member of the Government, though he exercised but little influence on the course of affairs, was liberated on that eventful day from the confinement to which his seditious proceedings against the Emperor during the previous winter had subjected him. The Empress Regent, refusing to resort to violence to uphold the Imperial Government, at once fled from the Tuileries, and, joining the Prince Imperial in Belgium, went with him to England, and settled down at Chiselhurst. The new government assumed the title of "Government of National Defence," and it was gradually recognized throughout the whole of France; though it is doubtful whether the country in general desired this change of Constitution. The Senate and the *Corps Législatif* met for the last time on the 4th of September.

The most important of the indirect results of this war was the annexation of Rome and the surrounding country to the dominions of Victor Emmanuel, thus completing the movement for Italian unity, begun in 1859–60. In itself, it was an event of considerable importance, and would have been so regarded, but that the Franco-German War engrossed the attention of Europe. The Popes had long claimed dominion over the city of Rome and a large portion of Italy, extending through the centre, from the Mediterranean to the Gulf of Venice, as their temporal sovereignty. These acquisitions, known as the States of the Church, they had obtained, by gift or otherwise, at various times in the Middle Ages, beginning with the reign of Pepin, King of France. The temporal, as well as the spiritual, authority of the Popes was great during the Middle

Ages, though they had been declining gradually since the Reformation.

In the movement which culminated in the union of the Italian peninsula into one kingdom under Victor Emmanuel (then King of Sardinia), in 1859-60, the eastern districts of the States of the Church joined the new monarchy, while the city of Rome and the adjoining territory remained under the dominion of the Pope. This was due, not to the attachment of the people to the temporal sovereignty of the Pope (for they were averse to it, and were strongly desirous of political union with the rest of Italy), but to the Emperor Napoleon III., who supported the pretensions of the reigning Pontiff, though the union of the rest of Italy was effected through his instrumentality. How much longer the temporal sovereignty would have stood if the Emperor Napoleon had remained on the throne cannot, of course, be known; though its eventual downfall was looked upon as certain.

The Revolution of the 4th of September hurled from power the man who had hitherto supported the Pope, and the temporal sovereignty, having no moral hold upon the people, at once fell, and resulted in the annexation of what remained of the Papal States to the Italian Kingdom. A popular vote was taken soon after, in which the annexation was ratified with great unanimity.

It was not until a year afterwards that the King of Italy entered Rome; but his troops took possession of the city in his name before the end of September, 1870, almost unopposed. The Italian Parliament held its first session in Rome in the course of the ensuing year.

The interest excited by the Franco-German War enabled Spain to choose and enthrone a king in comparative quiet. In view of the grave complications it had led to, Prince Leopold was not to be thought of; instead of a prince of the House of Hohenzollern,

Prince Amadeus, younger son of the King of Italy, was induced to reconsider his previous declination, and to become a candidate for the vacant throne. When the Cortes met, later in the autumn, to elect a sovereign, this prince received more than the requisite number of votes, and he was accordingly declared to be duly elected King of Spain. The King-elect took possession of his throne early in January, 1871, but General Prim, the man to whom he owed his throne, and who had been the virtual ruler of Spain ever since the Revolution of September, 1868, fell by an assassin's hand on Christmas Day, 1870, and expired from his wounds on New Year's Day, 1871. The new monarch, then only twenty-five or twenty-six years of age, was thus, at the commencement of his reign, thrown almost entirely on his own resources, in a country where, as a stranger, he must necessarily meet with much opposition to his government.

The surrender of the Emperor Napoleon had no effect in putting an end to the war, but rather prolonged it. The surrender, as we have stated, was followed by the downfall of the Regency, the proclamation of a Republic, and the establishment of a Provisional Government.

Their continued success exceeded the most sanguine hopes of the Germans, and thus enabled them, or rather encouraged them, to demand conditions of peace more favorable to themselves than they might otherwise have done. Peace might have been made at once after the capitulation of Sedan, had the Germans been content with more moderate terms, and had the French been in a state of mind to make peace.

The conditions of peace demanded by Count Bismarck at the time were the surrender of that part of France formerly known as Alsace and Lorraine, which had, nearly two centuries before, been wrested from a divided

Germany by France under Louis XIV., and which, in virtue of its Teutonic origin, he regarded as still the rightful possession of Germany, notwithstanding that, by means of the policy of the central government, and the intercourse of nearly two hundred years, the people had become intensely French, both in language and feeling. The payment of a war indemnity was demanded in addition. Jules Favre, Minister of Foreign Affairs under the Provisional Government, acted as ambassador on this occasion. He objected to the proposed terms as unjust, declaring that Europe would never sanction such a treaty, and he proposed an armistice of sufficient length for France to elect a National Assembly, which was to assume the government; this Assembly was also to be empowered to make a treaty with the Germans; Paris, and afterwards Tours, was named for its sittings. Bismarck at first refused to hear of an armistice; but he finally consented, on condition that the fortresses of Strasburg, Toul, Metz, and Phalsburg, should be delivered into the hands of the Germans, who were investing those places. These conditions being refused by the French, and the Germans refusing to make lighter terms, there was nothing to do but to continue the war. The French would probably have consented to these terms, hard as they were, could they have foreseen the fatal termination of the war, and the continued ill-fortune of their arms. Though his schemes were crowned with success, Count Bismarck lost for Germany, by his grasping demands, that sympathy that had been given her by the neutral public.

The Provisional Government established at Paris on September 4th received by degrees the sanction of the nation, as stated above, and was generally recognized by other Powers. Hopes were entertained that the establishment of republican institutions would rouse the energies of the people sufficiently to drive out the invader, though they were not destined to meet with the results that were anticipated.

Nevertheless, the change of government did not for a moment retard the progress of the Germans. No sooner was Sedan taken, and the ex-Emperor Napoleon on his way to Wilhelmshoehe, than the German armies continued their march towards the French capital; that is to say, such of the troops as were not necessary for the prosecution of the sieges then in progress. The Third and Fourth German Army Corps, under the command of the Crown Princes of Prussia and Saxony, struck off into the heart of France, and secretly wound their way to Paris where they arrived about the end of September. They numbered about 200,000 men. The King, accompanied by Von Moltke and Bismarck, led his army northwards, while Prince Frederic Charles, nicknamed the Red Prince, at the head of nearly 200,000 men, kept Marshal Bazaine and an army nearly equally large, shut up within the walls of Metz, for a while longer. The Grand Duke of Mecklenburg, at the head of an army corps, was investing Toul; while General Werder, with 60,000 under his command, was investing Strasburg. Toul was the first of these places to fall, and surrendered on the 28th of September. Nancy fell into the hands of the Germans on their way to Sedan.

The siege of Strasburg lasted about six weeks. This city is on the banks of the Rhine, opposite Kehl, in Baden, with which it was connected by a railway bridge; but this bridge was destroyed immediately after the outbreak of the war, by the Prussians. The siege was undertaken about the middle of August. The besieged city was heroically defended by the garrison during the six weeks the siege lasted under General Uhrich; during which time much harm was done to the city. Public as well as private buildings suffered in the siege. The Provisional

Government, shortly after its installation, sent a mayor to govern the city. He entered the town, after much difficulty, on September 22d, and he was at once recognized by General Uhrich. His administration, however, lasted only a week; for on the 28th, Strasburg was formally handed over to the Germans. The 17,000 troops who surrendered were sent into Germany, like those who surrendered at Sedan. Strasburg had been united to France for 189 years, almost to the very day.

The siege of Metz was still longer than that of Strasburg. A French army, under Marshal Bazaine, concentrated at Metz on August 10th, and the German army, on its approach, drove the French army into the town, and blockaded it there so closely that all efforts to raise the siege proved ineffective. Provisions became scarce: as to meat, there was none during the last two months of the siege; the place of meat was supplied by horseflesh. The cavalry horses were killed for the purpose, and the price of provisions became enormous. A few sorties were made by the French; but they proved unsuccessful. Bazaine refused to recognize the new government; but he continued his defence of Metz in the name of the Emperor. Finally, on October 27th, he signed a capitulation, surrendering himself and his whole army, 173,000 strong, including officers, into the hands of the Germans. The surrendered army was sent into Germany. Gambetta, in announcing this capitulation to the public, accused Bazaine of treachery. This charge was apparently believed by a vast majority of the French people; though it was evident that Bazaine surrendered only from sheer necessity.

Meanwhile, on September 21st, the German armies had completed the investment of Paris. The principal event of note on the way was the entry of the King of Prussia into Rheims, on September 5th, three days after the capitulation of Sedan. Two million inhabitants were now shut up in Paris. Comparatively few of these were native Parisians: the vast majority were Frenchmen, newly arrived from various parts of the country, who had fled to Paris for safety. Numbers of native Parisians left the city before the siege began, and took refuge in England. Of the two million at that time in Paris half a million were soldiers, many of whom were raw recruits.

General Trochu remained both the Civil and Military Governor of Paris during the siege: but so completely was Paris cut off from the rest of the world, that it was deemed necessary for the members of the Government to leave Paris, and to establish themselves elsewhere. Gambetta left by balloon on October 7th, and alighted at Tours, in the north of France (where three members of the Government had preceded him), which city became for a time the political capital of France.

The only means by which Paris could communicate with the outer world was by balloons and carrier-pigeons.

On October 5th, the King of Prussia, the Crown Prince, and the heads of the German armies, fixed their headquarters at Versailles. The King and the Crown Prince occupied the Palace of the Bourbons: a splendid palace, built by Louis XIV., one of the greatest of the Bourbons, but which will hereafter be associated with one of the darkest periods of French history. The Prussian headquarters continued to be at Versailles until the end of the war. The besiegers, though less numerous than the besieged army, had the advantage of thorough discipline on their side, and they derived additional advantage from the completeness with which they had succeeded in cutting off the communication of Paris with the rest of the country. Such troops as were not employed in the siege were occupied in overrunning the north of France. The great advantage of Paris lay in the length of its fortifications, which exceeded twenty-six miles, and in the vast number of troops enclosed within its walls, who, could they have been as well disciplined as their besiegers, might perhaps have raised the siege. The inhabitants of Paris remained sanguine of success until the end of the war.

Meanwhile, Gambetta, whose headquarters were now at Tours, monopolized the Government and was tacitly acknowledged by the nation as the chief ruler of France. By dint of great energy, he raised numerous, though undisciplined armies, and infused new hopes among the people; and for a time, he overshadowed all contemporary Frenchmen, except perhaps Trochu, who, as Governor of Paris, naturally attracted a great deal of attention. The French successes, small and few, proved only a momentary check to the progress of the German arms. Many of the Parisians were discontented with the course pursued by General Trochu, as they believed he did not make full use of the means at his command. The accusation against him was substantially the same as that made against Bazaine and MacMahon, and other French commanders who had been unable to resist the fate of war. How much truth there was in these accusations, it would be difficult to decide.

While the Germans occupied some of their troops in the investment of Paris, the remainder of their armies was employed in the north of France, where they received but temporary checks. Soon after the establishment of the Republic, Garibaldi, the Italian general, with a few troops under him, offered his services to the French Government, which were accepted. He caused much embarrassment to the enemy, by a sort of irregular warfare.

On October 11th, the German troops occupied Orleans. This city was recaptured by the army raised by

Gambetta while at Tours, on November 9th; the army was distinguished by the name of the Army of the Loire. It numbered two or three hundred thousand men, and was under the command of General d'Aurelle de Paladin. It was hoped by the French that this victory would be the turning-point of the war. The hope was doubtless due to the association of Orleans with Jeanne d'Arc, who, in the wars with the English, by the unexpected deliverance of this very city from the besiegers, turned the course of victory, by which means the invader was finally driven from the soil of France. But in this case the event did not answer the anticipations; the city was recaptured by the German invaders on December 4th, and remained in their hands until the end of the war.

The towns of Soissons and Schelestadt both surrendered before the end of October; Verdun, Neu-Breisach, Thionville, La Fère, and Amiens, all capitulated in the month of November.

Meanwhile, several sorties were attempted by the army besieged in Paris. The most important of these sorties was on the last day of November. Ninety thousand men, under the command of Trochu and Ducrot, left Paris, attacking the Wurtembergers and Saxons, and capturing Champigny, Brie, and Villiers. Another sortie was made on December 21st, in which the French were repulsed. A third great sortie was made on January 19th, of 100,000 men, under Generals Trochu and Ducrot, in which the French, after gaining some advantages, were obliged to retreat. As the closeness of the siege prevented all access to Paris, the famine necessarily increased. The supply of animals generally used for food finally ceased, and in their stead, the besieged made use of their war horses, dogs, and other animals. The mortality rose to a fearful rate, owing to the scarcity of even indifferent food.

About the middle of autumn, a movement began to be made in

Germany for crowning the gray-haired King of Prussia (he was then seventy-three years of age) Emperor of Germany. The same offer had been made to the King's brother, and predecessor, in 1848, but it was not accepted. The present King, however, accepted the imperial crown in December. The ceremony of inauguration, however, did not take place until January 18, 1871. This date had been chosen by the King on account of its being the anniversary of the day on which his ancestor, Frederic I., had mounted the throne of Prussia in 1700, changing his title from Elector of Brandenburg, which he had inherited from his own ancestors, for that of King of Prussia.

The ceremony of inaugurating William I., King of Prussia, as Emperor of Germany, took place in the Palace of the Bourbons, at Versailles, in the presence of the officers and flower of the German army, the German Parliament, and several of the German princes. It must have been a great humiliation to the French people, that the splendid palace built by one of her greatest monarchs should be rendered memorable as being the scene where a hostile sovereign ascended the throne of a new and powerful confederation on her borders.

This event was, in itself, one of historic importance. By this act the two Confederations of North and South Germany were formed into one, on the federal principle of a common parliament, a common army, diplomatic unity, etc., while the admission of the hereditary transmission of the crown was calculated to prevent the evils due to the elective principle of the former German Empire. The boundaries of the new Empire are not quite identical with those of the old one, seeing that they exclude German Austria and include non-German Prussia, being such provinces as Prussia acquired in the partition of Poland, and in which Polish is the common language. The annexation of Alsace and Lorraine made Germany rather larger than was France before the war. It is, of course, too soon as yet to pronounce the union of Germany in one state a success; but it is to be wished that this union should prove as completely successful as the friends of Germany could desire. It remains to be seen if it can stand the test of time, and whether it will survive the warriors and statesmen, many of whom are now far advanced in life, who were most instrumental in founding it.

We must now go back in our history as far as the recapture of Orleans by the Germans. On the day following the recapture, Count Von Moltke addressed the following note to General Trochu, sending it to him through a *parliamentaire*:

"VERSAILLES, Dec. 5th.

"It may be useful to inform your Excellency that the Army of the Loire was defeated yesterday near Orleans, and that the town is reoccupied by the

German troops. Should, however, your Excellency deem it expedient to be convinced of the fact through one of your own officers, I will not fail to provide him with a safe-conduct to come and return.

"Receive, General, the expression of the high consideration with which I have the honor to be, your very humble and obedient servant,

"The Chief of the Staff,
"Von Moltke."

General Trochu received the messenger affably, and brought the note the same day before the Council of Ministers for discussion. One of the Ministers thought that advantage ought to be taken of the occasion to discuss the possibilities of concluding an honorable peace; but the General urged that the Germans were in a hostile country in midwinter; that the late victory of the enemy might have been exaggerated; that help might come from the provinces; that

Paris might yet hold out for a considerable time; and that their arms might yet successfully end the war; therefore the war should be continued. At this time, great confidence was felt, both in the Army of the Loire, reputed to be two or three hundred thousand strong, and in the heroism of the people of Paris. The General's advice was accepted by the Council, and the following reply was accordingly sent to Von Moltke by the messenger:

"PARIS, Dec. 6th.

"Your Excellency thought it might be useful to inform me that the Army of the Loire was defeated near Orleans, and that the town is reoccupied by German troops.

"I have the honor to acknowledge the receipt of that communication, which I did not think expedient to verify through the means which your Excellency suggested to me.

"Receive, General, the expression

of the high consideration with which I have the honor to be,

"Your very humble and obedient servant,

"The Governor of Paris,
"General Trochu."

The only means of communication between Paris and the outer world during this period was by carrier-pigeons; though even this means was not to be relied on, as the pigeons would not fly after dark, and frequently they did not complete their journey, as they sometimes roosted overnight on the way: it was therefore necessary that they should be sent out at such an hour that they could reach their destination before sunset. They were frequently shot by sportsmen, their character as carrier-pigeons being unknown, or sometimes they would stop at a dove-cote, and leave their journey incomplete. The communications between Paris and the outer world were necessarily irregular. For some such reason, a message from Gambetta to the Governor of Paris did not reach the capital until six days after date. The message ran as follows:

"GAMBETTA TO JULES FAVRE AND TROCHU.

"BOURGES, Dec. 14th.

"During four days I have been here, occupied with Bourbaki, reorganizing the three Corps, the 15th, the 18th, and the 20th, of the Army of the Loire, severely cut up by the forced marches and the heavy rains following the evacuation of Orleans. This work will take some four or five more days to complete.

"The positions occupied by Bourbaki cover both Nevers and Bourges.

"The other portions of the Army, after the occupation of Orleans, retired on Beaugency, and Marchenoir: positions which it has retained against all the efforts of Frederic Charles, thanks to the great energy of General

Chanzy, whom recent events have shown to be a true man of war.

"The army, composed of the 16th, the 17th, and the 21st Corps, and supported by all the forces of the West, according to the orders of General Trochu, executed an admirable retreat, with very heavy losses to the Prussians. Chanzy stole away by a movement turning Frederic Charles on the left bank of the Loire at Blois and Amboise. Chanzy is in perfect security, ready to take the offensive against ——when his troops are rested, after having fought splendidly against superior numbers, from November 30th to December 12th.

"You thus see that the Army of the Loire is far from being destroyed according to the lies of the Prussians. It is separated into two equal forces, ready to operate, one on——the other ——so as to march on——."

This message seems to have been mutilated on the way, on account of the detention of the pigeons, and to have reached Paris in an incomplete form; and it ends, it will be seen, rather abruptly. Two armies were afterwards formed out of the Army of the Loire; they were called respectively the First and Second Army of the Loire. General Bourbaki was appointed commander-in-chief of the First, and General Chanzy, commander-in-chief of the Second of these armies.

On December 6th, the Prussian monarch issued this congratulatory address to his soldiers:

"SOLDIERS OF THE CONFEDERATE GERMAN ARMIES!

" We have again arrived at a crisis of the war. When I last addressed you, the last of the hostile armies which at the commencement of the campaign confronted us, had, by the capitulation of Metz, been destroyed. The enemy has since, by extraordinary exertions, opposed to us newly formed troops, and large portions of the inhabitants of France have forsaken their peaceful, and by us unhindered, vocations to take up arms. The enemy was frequently superior to us in numbers, but you have nevertheless again defeated him; for valor and discipline in a righteous cause are worth more than numerical preponderance. Every attempt on the part of the enemy to break through the investment lines of Paris have been firmly repulsed; often, indeed, with many bloody sacrifices, as at Champigny and at Le Bourget, but with a heroism such as you have everywhere displayed towards him. The armies of the enemy, which were advancing from every direction to the relief of Paris, have all been defeated. Our troops, some of whom only a few days ago stood before Metz and Strasburg, have to-day advanced as far as Orleans and Dijon, and, among many smaller engagements, two new important battles—that of Amiens and the several days' fight before Orleans—have been added to our former triumphs. Several fortresses have been conquered, and much war material has been taken. I have reason, therefore, for the greatest satisfaction, and it is to me a gratification and a duty to express this to you. I thank you all, from the general to the common soldier. Should the enemy persist in a further prosecution of the war, I know you will continue to show that exertion of all your powers to which we owe our great success hitherto, until we wring from him an honorable peace, worthy of the great sacrifices of blood and life which have been offered up.

"WILLIAM.

"HEADQUARTERS, VERSAILLES, December 6, 1870."

The French met with a small success in the capture of Ham, with 200 prisoners, on December 10th, but this was more than counterbalanced by the victories gained by the German armies about the same time. On December

8th, the Germans captured Beaugency, with 1100 prisoners and 6 guns, and on the 9th they captured Dieppe. Phalsburg surrendered, after a siege of several weeks' duration, on December 12th, its garrison of 1800 being taken prisoners by the German army. This was followed by the capture of Montmedy two days after by the Germans, with its garrison of 3000. General Chanzy, the commander-in-chief of the Second Army of the Loire, retired with his troops to the forest of Marchenoir. He was attacked at Vendôme and Freteval, and he was obliged to abandon both places on the 16th. On the last day of 1870, the Germans bombarded Mezières, capturing it on January 2, 1871, and taking 2000 prisoners. The Germans finally invested Le Mans on January 11th, and they entered the place the next day. This defeat effectually broke up the Army of the Loire. Prince Frederic Charles established his headquarters there on the 13th. Another French army, the Army of the North, under the command of Faidherbe, was broken up by a decisive defeat at St. Quentin.

We are now approaching the end of the war. Some German troops, commanded by Manteuffel, attacked the French on January 21st and 23d, and were repulsed. The Germans, however, captured Dole on the 21st, and Longni on the 24th, of the same month. About the same time, General Trochu resigned his powers as commander of the Paris troops in favor of General Vinoy (who had accompanied him in several of his sorties), retaining only his powers as President of the Council of Ministers.

But General Vinoy came into power too late to effect any good. The city of Paris had been reduced to such a state of distress by famine that it could hold out no longer; and on January 24th, M. Jules Favre was sent to Versailles to communicate with Count Bismarck concerning articles of peace.

The result was that an armistice was signed on January 28th, for a period of time extending to February 19th (subsequently extended to the 24th, and then to the 26th of the same month), to allow time for the election of a National Assembly, charged with full powers to make peace. The preliminary treaty was in the following terms:

"Between Count von Bismarck, Chancellor of the Germanic Confederation, stipulating in the name of his Majesty, the Emperor of Germany, King of Prussia, and M. Jules Favre, Minister of Foreign Affairs of the Government of National Defence, both furnished with regular powers, the following arrangements have been determined:

"ARTICLE I

"A general armistice over all the line of military operations in the course of being carried on between the German and French armies shall begin on this day: and for the Departments within the term of three days. The duration of the armistice shall be twenty-one days, dating from to-day; so that, unless it shall be renewed, the armistice will terminate on February 19th at noon. The belligerent armies will preserve their respective positions, which shall be separated by a line of demarcation. This line will commence from Pont Evêque on the coast of the Department of Calvados, and be continued upon Lignières, in the northeast of the Department of the Mayenne (passing between Briouze and Fromentel). Touching the Department at Lignières, it will follow the limit which separates that Department from the Department of the Orne, and of the Sarthe, to the north of Morannes, and will be continued in such a way as to leave in German occupation the Department of the Sarthe, Indre-et-Loire, Loire-et-Cher, and Yonne, as far as a point at which to the coast of Quarréles-Tombes, the Departments of the Côte d' Or, the Nièvre, and the Yonne, touch each other. Setting out from this point, the tracing of the line will be reserved for an understanding which shall take place as soon as the contracting parties shall be informed as to the actual state of the military operations which are being executed in the Department of the Côte d' Or, of the Doubs, and of the Jura. In any case, the line shall pass through the territory composed of these three Departments, leaving to German occupation the Departments situated to the north, and to the French army those situated to the south of this territory. The Departments of the North and of the Pas de Calais, the fortresses of Givet and Langres, with the territory which surrounds them to the distance of 10 kilometres, and the peninsula of Havre, as far as a line drawn from Étretat, in the direction of Romain, will remain outside the limits of German occupation. The two belligerent armies, and their advanced posts on either side, will remain at a distance of 10 kilometres from the lines drawn to separate their positions. Each of the two armies reserves for itself the right of maintaining its authority in the territory that it occupies, and of employing the means which its commander may judge necessary to attain that end. The armistice applies equally to the naval forces of the two countries, adopting the meridian of Dunkerque as the line of demarcation, to the west of which the French fleet will remain, and to the east of which, as soon as they can be warned, will withdraw those German ships of war which are westward of that line. The captures which are made after the conclusion, and before the notification, of the armistice, will be restored, as well as the prisoners who may be taken in the period indicated. The military operations in the territory of the Departments of Doubs, Jura, and Côte d' Or, as well as the siege of Belfort shall continue independently of the armistice, until an agreement shall be arrived at regarding the line of demarcation, the tracing of which through the three Departments mentioned has been reserved for an ulterior understanding.

"ARTICLE II.

"The armistice thus agreed upon has been made so as to permit the Government of National Defence to convoke an Assembly, freely elected, which will pronounce upon the question whether the war shall be continued, or on what conditions peace shall be made. The Assembly will meet in the city of Bordeaux. Every facility will be given by the commanders of the German armies for the elections and the meeting of the Deputies who compose that Assembly.

"ARTICLE III.

"There shall be immediately surrendered to the German army by the French military authorities all the forts forming the perimeters of the exterior defence of Paris, as well as their material of war. The communes and the houses situated outside that perimeter, or between the forts, may be occupied by the German troops as far as a line to be drawn by military commissioners. The ground between this line and the fortified *enceinte* of the city of Paris will be interdicted to the armed forces of the two sides. The manner of surrendering the forts, and the drawing of the line already mentioned, will form the object of a protocol to be annexed to the present convention.

"ARTICLE IV.

"During the armistice the German army will not enter the city of Paris.

"ARTICLE V.

"The *enceinte* shall be disarmed of its guns, the carriages of which will be transported into the forts designated for that purpose by a commission of the German army.

"ARTICLE VI.

"The garrisons (Army of the Line, Mobile Guard, and Marine), of the forts of Paris shall be prisoners of war, excepting a division of 12,000 men, which the military authorities will preserve for service inside the city. The troops who are prisoners of war shall lay down their arms, which will be collected in the places designated, and given up, according to arrangements made by a commissioner, in the usual manner. These troops shall remain in the interior of the city, where they will not be allowed to pass the *enceinte* during the armistice. The French authorities bind themselves to take care that every individual belonging to the army and to the Mobile Guard shall remain in the interior of the town. The officers of the captured troops shall be designated in a list to be delivered to the German authorities. At the expiration of the armistice, all the combatants of the army confined in Paris will have leave to constitute themselves prisoners of war to the German army, if before that time peace is not concluded. The officers made prisoners will retain their arms.

"Article VII.

"The National Guard will retain its arms. It will be charged with the protection of Paris and maintenance of order. The same will be the case with the gendarmerie, and the assimilated troops employed in the municipal service, such as the Republican Guard, the Douaniers, and the Pompiers. The whole of this category shall not exceed 3500. All the Corps of Franc-Tireurs shall be dissolved by ordinance of the French Government.

"Article VIII.

"Immediately after the signatures of these presents, and before the taking possession of the forts, the commander-in-chief of the German armies will give every facility to the commissioners whom the French Government will send, whether into the Departments or abroad, to take steps for the revictualling of, and the bringing to, the city the commodities which are destined for it.

"ARTICLE IX.

"After the surrender of the forts, and after the disarmament of the *enceinte* and of the garrison, stipulated in Articles V. and VI., there victualling of Paris will be effected freely by transit upon the railroads and the rivers. Provisions intended for this revictualling shall not be drawn from the districts occupied by the German troops: and the French Government engages itself to obtain provisions outside of the line of demarcation which surrounds the positions of the German armies, except in the case of an authorization to the contrary effect given by the commander of the latter.

"Article X.

"Every person wishing to quit the city of Paris must be furnished with regular permits, delivered by the French military authority and submitted to the *visé* of the German authorities. Permits, or *visés*, will be granted, in right of their position, to candidates, to the provincial deputations, and to the deputies of the Assembly. The free movements of the persons who have received the authorization indicated will be permitted only between six in the morning and six in the evening.

"Article XI.

"The city of Paris shall pay a municipal contribution of war amounting to 200,000,000 francs [$40,000,000 United States currency]. The payment must be effected before the fifteenth day of the armistice: the mode of payment to be determined by a mixed German and French commission.

"Article XII.

" During the armistice nothing shall be taken away from the public objects of value which may serve as pledges for the recovery of war contributions.

"Article XIII.

" The transport into Paris of arms, of munitions of war, or of articles entering into their manufacture, is forbidden during the terms of the armistice.

"Article XIV.

" Immediate steps shall be taken for the exchange of all prisoners of war made by the French army since the commencement of the war. For this end the French authorities will hand, as promptly as possible, nominal lists of the German prisoners of war to the German authorities at Amiens, at Le Mans, at Orleans, and at Vesoul. The liberation of the German prisoners of war will be effected at the points nearest to the frontier. The German authorities will deliver in exchange, at the same points, and in the briefest possible time, to the French military authorities, a like number of French prisoners of war, of corresponding grades. The exchange will extend to civil prisoners, such as captains of ships of the German merchant navy, and the civilian French prisoners who have been kept in Germany.

"ARTICLE XV.

"A postal service for letters not sealed will be organized between Paris and the Departments through the medium of the headquarters at Versailles. In faith of which the undersigned have appended to the present Convention their signatures and their seals.

"Done at Versailles, the 28th of January, 1871.

"[L.S.] BISMARCK. [L.S.] FAVRE."

This convention was signed without consultation with Gambetta and the delegates of the Government, who were now sitting in Bordeaux, instead of in Tours. M. Gambetta at first deemed it incredible that the delegates of the Government in Paris should have surrendered the city without consultation with those in Bordeaux; but, when the official despatches by Jules Favre were received, Gambetta issued a proclamation to this effect:

"Paris the impregnable, forced and vanquished by famine, has succumbed, but the city remains intact, as a last homage wrested by the power of moral grandeur from the barbarians: but, as if our ill-fortune had resolved to crush us, something more sinister and painful than the fall of Paris has come upon us. Unknown to us, without informing us, and without consulting us, an armistice has been signed of which we have too late learned the guilty thoughtlessness, which surrenders to the Prussian troops Departments occupied by our soldiers, and imposes upon us the obligation to remain inactive three weeks, in order to convoke a National Assembly, in the sad circumstances in which our country is placed."

Gambetta, however, ratified the armistice convention: but he attempted to insure the election of Republicans to the Assembly, by a decree in which he declared ineligible all persons who had filled the posts of Minister, Senator, Councillor of State, or Prefect under the late Empire, or who had accepted official candidatures. He also declared ineligible all members of the different dynasties who had reigned over France. His colleagues, however, revoked the decree, and restored freedom of election; whereupon Gambetta resigned his functions, declaring that he and his colleagues had no hopes in common. The members of the Government replied to Gambetta's reproaches by the following decree:

"We do not admit that arbitrary restrictions can be imposed upon the ballot. We have fought against the Empire and its practices, and we do not intend to revive them by instituting a system of official candidatures by means of elimination. Great mistakes may have been committed, and heavy responsibilities may flow therefrom : nothing can be more true than that the misfortunes of the country efface everything but its extreme need; and, moreover, by lowering ourselves to the condition of mere party actors, to proscribe our former antagonists, we should have the shame and sorrow of wounding those who have fought and bled by our sides. To recall the memory of past dissensions at a time when the enemy treads our blood-stained soil, is to retard by our rancors the great task of the deliverance of our country. We regard principles as superior to expedients. We do not wish that the first decree of the Republican Assembly in 1871 should be an act of mistrust directed against the electors. To them belongs the sovereignty : let them exercise it without weakness, and the country will be saved."

The elections took place on February 8th. Owing to the short time allowed, which scarcely permitted deliberation, or communication between the different parts of France, it was found when the Assembly met, that the same member was often elected by two or more constituencies, which rendered supplementary elections afterwards necessary. M. Gambetta was chosen by several constituencies. M. Thiers was evidently the most popular of the members, being chosen by about twenty-five different constituencies. Alsace and Lorraine sent members, who withdrew after the ratification of peace.

The National Assembly met in the theatre at Bordeaux on February 12th. The desire for peace being uppermost among the people at this moment, members of various political hues were elected, and the Assembly was composed of moderate men. The day after the Assembly met Jules Favre, in the name of his colleagues and himself, resigned the powers of the Government of National Defence into the hands of that body; he announced, however, that they would remain at their posts until their successors were appointed. He spoke as follows:

"We have borne the burden of government; but we have no other desire, under existing circumstances, than to be able to place our temporary plans in the hands of the National Assembly. Thanks to your patriotism and reunion, we hope that the country, having been taught by misfortune, will know how to heal her wounds, and to reconstitute the national existence. We no longer have any power. We depend entirely upon your decision.

We confidently expect the constitution of new and legitimate powers."

Garibaldi, on the same day, resigned his seat in the Assembly, and he shortly afterwards left for his home in the island of Caprera. On the 16th, the Assembly organized by electing M. Grévy, a moderate Republican, as its President. M. Thiers was the next day elected Chief of the Executive Power. He assumed at once the functions of his office, and proceeded to appoint a Cabinet. A protest against the proposed annexation of Alsace and Lorraine to Germany was laid by the deputies of those provinces before the House; it ran as follows:

"The National Assembly, France and Europe, which are witnesses to the exactions of Prussia, cannot permit the completion of an act which would rend Alsace and Lorraine from France. We are, and will forever remain, French, in good as well as in evil fortune. We have sealed with our own blood the indissoluble pact which unites us to France; and we affirm once more, in the depths of all our trials, our immovable loyalty to the Fatherland. France cannot abandon those who will not be separated from her. The National Assembly, sprung from universal suffrage, could not concede demands tending to destroy the nationality of a whole population. Neither can the people, in its electoral colleges, allow it. As little can Europe confirm these criminal attempts, and let a whole people be treated like a herd of tame beasts. Peace, in consideration of the cession of territory, can never be a durable peace, but merely a momentary truce, soon to be followed by another war. As to ourselves, inhabitants of Alsace and Lorraine, we are ready to resume fighting, and therefore we shall hold as null and void any offer, treaty, vote, and *plebiscite* which would have for its object the separation of Alsace and Lorraine from France. We proclaim our right to remain united to French soil, and we formally engage ourselves to defend our honor."

After some discussion, the Assembly decided that M. Thiers should be left free to sign such terms of peace as the Germans would agree to. It was a task of some difficulty, as Bismarck was stringent, and would not yield one iota of the German claims. Nevertheless, on February 26th, the treaty was signed at Versailles, and was finally ratified by the Assembly. On February 28th, M. Thiers arrived at Bordeaux from Versailles, and at once submitted the following bill for the approval of the Assembly.

"The National Assembly, forced by necessity, and therefore not being responsible, adopts the Preliminaries of Peace signed at Versailles on February 26th.

"ART. I. France renounces in

favor of the German Empire the following rights : The whole of Lorraine, including Metz and Thionville, and Alsace, but without Belfort.

"ART. II. France will pay the sum of five milliards of francs, of which one milliard is to be paid in 1871, and the remaining four milliards by instalments extending over three years.

"ART. III. The German troops will begin to evacuate the French territory as soon as the treaty is ratified. They will first evacuate the interior of Paris, and some Departments lying in the western region. The evacuations of the other Departments will take place gradually after payment of the first milliard, and proportionally to the payment of the other milliards. Interest of five per cent. will be paid on the amount remaining due from the date of the ratification of the treaty.

"ART. IV. The German troops will not levy any requisitions in the Departments occupied by them : but, on the other hand, they will be maintained at the cost of France.

"ART. V. A delay will be granted to the inhabitants of the territories annexed to decide for themselves severally to which of the two nationalities they will adhere.

"ART. VI. Prisoners of war will be immediately set at liberty.

"ART. VII. Negotiations for a definite treaty of peace will be opened at Brussels after the ratification of the treaty.

"ART. VIII. The administration of the Departments occupied by the German troops will be entrusted to French officials, but under the control of the chiefs of the German corps of occupation.

"ART. IX. The present treaty confers on the Germans no rights whatever in the portion of territory not occupied.

"ART. X. The treaty will have to be ratified by the National Assembly of France."

The time of paying the five milliards

was afterwards lengthened a year, until March, 1875.

Intense excitement was caused in Paris by the report that the Germans intended to enter the city. In order to allay this excitement, M. Thiers issued the following proclamation :

"INHABITANTS OF PARIS!

" The Government appeals to your patriotism and wisdom. You have in your hands the fate of Paris. Upon you it depends to save or destroy France herself. After a heroic resistance, famine compelled us to give up the forts to the victorious enemy. The army which we had hoped would be able to help us was driven back beyond the Loire, and incontestable facts obliged the Government and the National Assembly to open negotiations. During six days the negotiators fought foot by foot, and did what was humanly possible to obtain the most favorable conditions, and have signed the preliminaries, which will be ceded to Germany. Five milliards are to be paid, and portions of France are to remain occupied until the amount is paid. Paris will be partially occupied if the ratification at Bordeaux follows. We are now at the end of a glorious but bloody war, which was forced upon us with frivolity without parallel, and in which your troops have taken so honorable a part. May the greatness of Germany be consolidated in peace."

On March 1st, some 30,000 Prussian and Bavarian troops, with some of the German princes at their head, entered Paris; but the treaty being ratified that day, they evacuated it on the 2d. Neither the Emperor nor the Crown Prince were among them. The German army immediately began to evacuate the French territory, leaving only such troops as were necessary for the occupation of several of the French Departments, until the payment of the war indemnity.

The ex-Emperor Napoleon left his confinement at Wilhelmshoehe about the middle of March, and joined his wife and son at Chiselhurst, in the south of England, where they have since resided in strict privacy.

The French Assembly shortly afterwards transferred its sittings to Versailles, which has since been the political capital of France. About the same time M. Thiers was elected President of the Republic for a period of three years.

Here I must close my history. The war led to changes more important than at first foreseen; and whether these changes will be lasting and beneficial, time alone can show. Meanwhile, I lay down my pen.

FINIS.

www.ingramcontent.com/pod-product-compliance
Lightning Source LLC
Chambersburg PA
CBHW022139160426
43197CB00009B/1359